# Collins

# Grammar, Punctuation and Vocabulary Progress Tests

Year 6/P7

Author:
**Rachel Clarke**

Series editor:
**Stephanie Austwick**

William Collins' dream of knowledge for all began with the publication of his first book in 1819. A self-educated mill worker, he not only enriched millions of lives, but also founded a flourishing publishing house. Today, staying true to this spirit, Collins books are packed with inspiration, innovation and practical expertise. They place you at the centre of a world of possibility and give you exactly what you need to explore it.

Collins. Freedom to teach.

Published by Collins
An imprint of HarperCollins*Publishers*
The News Building
1 London Bridge Street
London SE1 9GF

Browse the complete Collins catalogue at www.collins.co.uk

© HarperCollins*Publishers* Limited 2019

10 9 8 7 6 5 4 3 2 1

ISBN 978-0-00-833366-9

All rights reserved. No part of this publication may be reproduced, stored in a retrieval system, or transmitted in any form by any means, electronic, mechanical, photocopying, recording or otherwise, without the prior written permission of the Publisher or a licence permitting restricted copying in the United Kingdom issued by the Copyright Licensing Agency Ltd., Barnard's Inn, 86 Fetter Lane, London, EC4A 1EN.

British Library Cataloguing in Publication Data. A catalogue record for this publication is available from the British Library.

Author: Rachel Clarke

Series Editor and Reviewer: Stephanie Austwick

Publisher: Katie Sergeant

Product Manager: Sarah Thomas

Content Editor: Holly Woolnough

Copyeditor and proofreader: Tanya Solomons

Internal design and typesetting: Hugh Hillyard-Parker

Cover designers: The Big Mountain Design and Ken Vail Graphic Design

Production Controller: Katharine Willard

# Contents

How to use this book   4

Year 6 Curriculum map: Yearly overview   6

**Year 6/P7 Half Termly Tests**

Autumn Half Term 1   7
Autumn Half Term 2   21
Spring Half Term 1   34
Spring Half Term 2   46
Summer Half Term 1   59
Summer Half Term 2   73

**Mark schemes**

Autumn Half Term 1   86
Autumn Half Term 2   89
Spring Half Term 1   92
Spring Half Term 2   95
Summer Half Term 1   98
Summer Half Term 2   101

Record sheet   104

# How to use this book

## Introduction

Collins *Grammar, Punctuation and Vocabulary Progress Tests* have been designed to give you a consistent whole-school approach to teaching and assessing grammar, punctuation and vocabulary. Each photocopiable book covers the required vocabulary, grammar and punctuation objectives from the English National Curriculum statutory guidance and vocabulary, grammar and punctuation appendix. For teachers in Scotland, the books can offer guidance and structure that is not provided in the Curriculum for Excellence Experiences and Outcomes or Benchmarks.

Revision of previous years' work is also included, where appropriate, to ensure children are building their skills to become confident and secure users of grammar, punctuation and vocabulary. As standalone tests, independent of any teaching and learning scheme, the Collins *Grammar, Punctuation and Vocabulary Progress Tests* provide a structured way to assess progress in grammar, punctuation and vocabulary, to help you identify areas for development, and to provide evidence towards expectations for each year group.

## Building confidence and understanding

At the end of Key Stage 1 and Key Stage 2, children are assessed on their understanding of grammar, punctuation and vocabulary. This is done through teacher assessment of children's writing, through the grammar, punctuation and vocabulary SAT in KS2 and through the optional SAT in KS1. Collins *Grammar, Punctuation and Vocabulary Progress Tests* have been designed to help children recognise grammatical features whilst building familiarity with the format, language and style of the SATs. Through regular use of the Collins *Grammar, Punctuation and Vocabulary Progress Tests* children should develop and practise the necessary skills to complete the national tests confidently and proficiently.

The Collins *Grammar, Punctuation and Vocabulary Progress Tests* are written so that new grammatical content is presented in a variety of ways with increasing challenge over the tests in the book. Previous learning is also addressed in Years 2 – 6 with questions that ask children to recall grammar, punctuation and vocabulary learned in previous year groups.

## How to use this book

In this book, you will find six photocopiable half-termly tests, written to replicate the format of the SATs with space for children to write their answers. You will also find a Curriculum Map on page 6 indicating the aspects of the Content Domain covered in each test and across the year group. These have been cross-referenced with the appropriate age-related statements from the National Curriculum. In KS2, each test should take 35 – 45 minutes to complete and in KS1 each test should take approximately 20 minutes. KS1 teachers may prefer to administer each test in two halves of 10 minutes each, and in Year 1 read each question to children.

To help you mark the tests, you will find mark schemes that include the number of marks to be awarded, model answers and a reference to the elements of the Content Domain covered by each question.

## Test demand

The tests have been written to ensure smooth progression in children's understanding of grammar, punctuation and vocabulary within the book and across the rest of the books in the series. Each test builds on those before it so that children are guided towards the expectations of the SATs at the end of KS1 and KS2.

Year 6: How to use this book

| Year group | Number of marks per test |
|---|---|
| 1 | 20 |
| 2 | 20 |
| 3 | 30 |
| 4 | 30 |
| 5 | 40 |
| 6 | 50 |

## Performance thresholds

The table below provides guidance for assessing how children perform in the tests. Most children should achieve scores at or above the expected standard with some children working at greater depth and exceeding expectations for their year group. Whilst these threshold bands do not represent standardised scores, as in the end of key stage SATs, they will give an indication of how children are performing against the expected standard for their year group.

| Year group | Working towards | Expected standard | Greater depth |
|---|---|---|---|
| 1 | 9 marks or below | 10–16 marks | 17–20 marks |
| 2 | 9 marks or below | 10–16 marks | 17–20 marks |
| 3 | 14 marks or below | 15–25 marks | 26–30 marks |
| 4 | 14 marks or below | 15–25 marks | 26–30 marks |
| 5 | 18 marks or below | 19–33 marks | 34–40 marks |
| 6 | 23 marks or below | 24–42 marks | 43–50 marks |

## Tracking progress

A record sheet is provided to help you illustrate to children the areas in which they have performed well and where they need to develop. A spreadsheet tracker is also provided via collins.co.uk/assessment/downloads which enables you to identify whole-class patterns of attainment. This can then be used to inform your next teaching and learning steps.

## Editable download

All the files are available in Word and PDF format for you to edit if you wish. Go to collins.co.uk/assessment/downloads to find instructions on how to download. The files are password protected and the password clue is included on the website. You will need to use the clue to locate the password in your book. You can use these editable files to help you meet the specific needs of your class, whether that be by increasing or decreasing the challenge, by reducing the number of questions, by providing more space for answers or increasing the size of text as required for specific children.

© HarperCollinsPublishers Ltd 2019

# Year 6 Curriculum map: Yearly overview

| National Curriculum objective (Year 6) | Content domain | Autumn Test 1 | Autumn Test 2 | Spring Test 1 | Spring Test 2 | Summer Test 1 | Summer Test 2 |
|---|---|---|---|---|---|---|---|
| **WORD** | | | | | | | |
| The difference between vocabulary typical of informal speech and vocabulary appropriate for formal speech and writing [for example, *find out – discover, ask for – request, go in – enter, said – reported*] | G7 | ● | | | | | ● |
| How words are related by meaning as synonyms and antonyms [for example, *big, large, little*] | G6 | ● | | ● | ● | ● | ● |
| **SENTENCE** | | | | | | | |
| Use of the passive for presentation of information in a sentence [for example, *I broke the window in the greenhouse* versus *The window in the greenhouse was broken (by me)*] | G4 | | | ● | | ● | ● |
| The difference between structures typical of informal speech and structures appropriate for formal speech and writing [for example, the use of question tags: *He's your friend, isn't he?*, or the use of subjunctive forms such as *If I were* or *Were they to come* in some very formal writing and speech] | G7 | | ● | | ● | | ● |
| **PUNCTUATION** | | | | | | | |
| Use of the semi-colon, colon and dash to mark the boundary between independent clauses [for example, *It's raining; I'm fed up*] | G5 | ● | ● | | ● | | ● |
| Use of the colon to introduce a list and use of semi-colons within lists | G5 | ● | ● | ● | ● | ● | ● |
| Punctuation of bullet points to list information | G5 | | ● | | ● | | ● |
| How hyphens can be used to avoid ambiguity [for example, *man eating shark* versus *man-eating shark*, or *recover* versus *re-cover*] | G5 | | | | ● | | |

Content Domain Key
G1: Grammatical terms / word clauses
G2: Functions of sentences
G3: Combining words, phrases and clauses
G4: Verb forms, tenses and consistency
G5: Punctuation
G6: Vocabulary
G7: Standard English and formality

| Name: | Year: | Date: |

# Autumn Half Term 1

**1** Circle each word that should begin with a **capital letter** in the sentence below.

I am inviting these people to my party: sophie, lottie, amal and jo.

1 mark

**2** Circle the **subordinating conjunction** in the sentence below.

We like to eat fish and chips when we go to the seaside.

1 mark

**3** Tick **one** box in each row to show whether each sentence uses **capital letters** correctly.

| Sentence | Correct | Incorrect |
|---|---|---|
| On Saturday, seema is going to Birmingham. | | |
| Cassie is going to glasgow in June. | | |
| Jamal went to Cardiff last summer. | | |

2 marks

**4** Circle all the **determiners** in the sentence below.

Inside the drawer, I found an old coin, a ball of string and a pair of rusty scissors.

1 mark

**5** Insert an **apostrophe** in the correct place in the sentence below.

Mrs Browns dog has a loud bark.

1 mark

**6** Which option is punctuated correctly?

Tick **one**.

"Let's play skipping at break time" said Shaz ☐

"Let's play skipping at break time," Said Shaz. ☐

"Let's play skipping at break time," said Shaz. ☐

"Let's play skipping," at break time said Shaz. ☐

1 mark

**7** Write words formed using the **suffix -ate** to complete these sentences.

I checked my work to ensure that my answers were _____.

My little brother is very _____ and likes to give us all cuddles.

1 mark

**8** Insert the missing **punctuation mark** to complete the sentence below.

What would you like to do when you grow up

1 mark

**9** Which punctuation mark should be used in the space indicated by the arrow?

S e b s  h a m s t e r  w a s  h i d i n g  u n d e r  a  c h a i r.
   ↑

Tick **one**.

question mark ☐

exclamation mark ☐

comma ☐

apostrophe ☐

1 mark

**10** Add **two full stops** in the correct places in the passage below.

It's my birthday on Friday I am going to have a party with cake and balloons

1 mark

**11** Circle the **conjunction** in the sentence below.

I love English lessons because I like writing stories.

1 mark

**12** Choose the correct word to complete each sentence.
Write the word on the line.

I made _____ pancake with my big brother Josh.

a / an

We mixed some flour, half a pint of milk and _____ egg in a bowl.

a / an

Then we cooked the mixture in _____ frying pan.

a / an

1 mark

**13** Which option correctly completes the sentence below?

Mr Jones wanted to know _____ was going on the school trip.

Tick **one**.

who's ☐

whose ☐

whom ☐

who ☐

1 mark

**14** Tick **one** box in each row to show whether the **possessive apostrophe** has been used correctly or incorrectly.

| Sentence | Correct | Incorrect |
| --- | --- | --- |
| Dads magazine is about car's. | | |
| I borrowed Joe's pencil. | | |
| Amit's mum is a nurse. | | |

2 marks

**15** Insert a **pair of brackets** in the correct place in the sentence below.

The Eiffel Tower in Paris is 324 metres tall.

1 mark

**16** Tick **one** box in each row to show whether the underlined word is **plural** or **possessive**.

| Sentence | Plural | Possessive |
| --- | --- | --- |
| The dog's basket is in the kitchen. | | |
| I practised my spellings last night. | | |
| The children put their books in their bags. | | |

2 marks

**17** Create a **bullet-pointed list** for these ingredients: apples, bananas and grapes.
Remember to punctuate your answer correctly.

To make a fruit salad, you will need these ingredients:

1 mark

**18** Draw a line to match each sentence to the correct **determiner**.
Use each determiner only once.

| Sentence | Determiner |
|---|---|
| Sam gave me _____ sweet. | an |
| It was _____ tastiest sweet in the world. | the |
| Now I've got _____ achy tooth. | a |

1 mark

**19** Which sentence uses a **possessive apostrophe** correctly?

Tick **one**.

Gus went to Grans' house on Sunday. ☐

Gus' went to Gran's house on Sunday. ☐

Gus went to Gran's house on Sunday. ☐

Gus' went to Grans house on Sunday. ☐

*1 mark*

**20** Circle the correct word to complete the sentence below.

The cat's / cats ate their dinner then went to sleep.

*1 mark*

**21** Circle the **relative pronoun** in the sentence below.

The library, which was run by Mr Siddiqi, was full of books.

*1 mark*

**22** Add the correct punctuation to the sentence below.

Ali said I would like to play football on Saturday.

*1 mark*

**23** Complete the sentence below with a **modal verb** to show possibility.

Dara _____ go to the cinema this evening.

*1 mark*

**24** Tick the sentence that indicates the greatest certainty that it will stop snowing soon.

Tick **one**.

It will possibly stop snowing soon. ☐

It will maybe stop snowing soon. ☐

It will probably stop snowing soon. ☐

It will definitely stop snowing soon. ☐

1 mark

**25** Rewrite the sentence below as **direct speech**. Remember to punctuate your sentence correctly.

I said that I am going to visit my granny on Sunday.

_____

1 mark

**26** Complete the sentence below with a **verb** formed from the adjective <u>equal</u>.

The netball team needed one more goal to _____ the score with the other team.

1 mark

**27** Underline the **relative clause** in the sentence below.

I have a big sister who is a police officer.

1 mark

**28** Insert a **semi-colon** in the correct place in the sentence below.

There is a huge field near our school; it is being ploughed tomorrow.

1 mark

**29** Circle the correct **modal verb** to complete the sentences below.

Mrs Lall said, "The cross-country route is hard, but I am sure you can / may finish it."

"Please Sir, may / can I have a drink of water?" asked Sasha.

In our class, if you finish all your work, you can / may choose a comic to read.

1 mark

**30** Write the name of punctuation that could be used instead of **commas** in the sentence below.

Today, despite feeling unwell, I wrote two whole pages in my writing book.

_____

1 mark

**31** Which sentence is the most **formal**?

Tick **one**.

The internet is great for learning about insects. ☐

I learned stuff about insects on the internet. ☐

I used the internet to discover more about insects. ☐

You can learn loads about insects on the internet. ☐

1 mark

**32** Which sentence is about three foods?

Tick **one**.

We had chicken, pizza and ice cream for dinner. ☐

We had chicken pizza and ice cream for dinner. ☐

1 mark

**33** Write the name of punctuation that could be used instead of **brackets** in the sentence below.

Mr Howe (a teacher at our school) plays football at the weekends.

_____

1 mark

**34** Tick the sentence that uses a **dash** correctly.

Tick **one**.

I find jigsaws tricky – there are so many pieces. ☐

I find jigsaws tricky there are – so many pieces. ☐

I find jigsaws – tricky there are so many pieces. ☐

I find jigsaws tricky there – are so many pieces. ☐

1 mark

**35** Which **noun** is a **synonym** of the noun underline{journey}?

Tick **one**.

fall ☐
trip ☐
flight ☐
drive ☐

1 mark

**36** Circle the correct **adverb of possibility** to complete the sentence below.

It's very cold and windy in the arctic so you definitely / maybe need to wear a coat.

1 mark

**37** In which sentence is Ella imagining Jimmy was a frog?

Tick **one**.

Ella imagined Jimmy was a frog. ☐
Ella, imagined Jimmy, was a frog. ☐

1 mark

**38** Which sentence is the most **formal**?

Tick **one**.

My parents request that you attend my party. ☐
You would like to come to my party, wouldn't you? ☐
I'd love you to join me for my party. ☐
I'm having a party – please come! ☐

1 mark

**39** Circle the **two** words that are **antonyms** in the sentence below.

In London you can see a fascinating range of buildings including ancient churches and modern office blocks.

1 mark

**40** Which one **prefix** can be added to all three words below to make their **antonyms**?
Write the prefix in the box.

legal
legible
logical

1 mark

**41** Tick **one** box to show the correct place for a **semi-colon** in the sentence below.

Tick **one**.
The weather was windy leaves flew through the air.

1 mark

**42** Circle the most **formal** option in each box to complete the invitation.

The head teacher [ asks / requests / begs ] that you attend a presentation evening to [ recognise / show / show off ] the [ work / achievements / attempts ] of your child.

2 marks

**43** Tick **one** box in each row to show whether the underlined word is **plural** or **possessive**.

| Sentence | Plural | Possessive |
| --- | --- | --- |
| The giraffe's neck is very long. | | |
| A lion's mane is extremely furry. | | |
| The elephants wandered across the savannah. | | |

2 marks

**44** a) Write an explanation of the word **synonym**.

_____

_____

1 mark

b) Write one word that is a **synonym** of underline{untidy}.

_____

_____

1 mark

Total: _____ /50

Name:        Year:        Date:

# Autumn Half Term 2

**1** Circle each word that should begin with a **capital letter** in the sentence below.

The countries that make up the united kingdom are: england, scotland, wales and northern ireland.

1 mark

**2** Circle the correct word to show that there is only one dog.

The dog's / dogs' dinner was put in a large bowl.

1 mark

**3** Rewrite the sentence below using the **present progressive** tense.

Miss Reed tidies the school library.

_____

1 mark

**4** Write the correct word in the box in the sentence below.

     unfriendly     friendship     friend

Zac and Hamish had known each other for five years. Their ☐ began when they were in Year 1.

1 mark

Year 6: Autumn Half Term Test 2

**5** Rewrite the sentence below so that it has a **fronted adverbial**.

Class 6 had Maths after lunch.

_____

1 mark

**6** Which sentence is grammatically correct?

Tick **one**.

George done the dusting. ☐

Jayesh were washing the dishes. ☐

We was all helping with the housework. ☐

Archie did the watering. ☐

1 mark

**7** Circle each word that should begin with a **capital letter** in the sentence below.

evan thomas is a pupil at smalltown primary school.

1 mark

**8** Which sentence is in **Standard English**?

Tick **one**.

I went to the football match with my uncle. ☐

I been to town with my cousin. ☐

We seen a clown at the circus. ☐

I've already did my homework today. ☐

1 mark

**9** Rewrite the sentence below in the **past progressive**. Remember to punctuate your answer correctly.

Callum is trying to read his book.

_____

1 mark

**10** Tick the option that shows how the underlined words in the sentence below are used.

Earlier today, we played tennis.

|  | Tick **one**. |
|---|---|
| as a main clause | ☐ |
| as a fronted adverbial | ☐ |
| as a subordinate clause | ☐ |
| as a noun phrase | ☐ |

1 mark

**11** Which one **prefix** can be added to all three words below to make their **antonyms**?
Write the prefix in the box.

correct
visible
active

[          ]

1 mark

**12** Which option completes the sentence in the **present perfect tense**?

Jonny and Suki _____ chess at school today.

Tick **one**.

has played ☐

have played ☐

played ☐

play ☐

1 mark

**13** Tick **one** box in each row to show whether the underlined noun is **singular** or **plural**.

| Sentence | Singular | Plural |
|---|---|---|
| The teachers' mugs were in the staffroom. | | |
| The princess's crowns were covered in jewels. | | |
| Those are the girls' toys. | | |

2 marks

**14** Rewrite the sentence below in **Standard English**.

Gurdip done the drawing.

_____

1 mark

**15** Tick to show where a **colon** should be used to introduce a list.

Tick **one**.

These are my best friends Gemma, Grace and Sangeeta.
   ↑        ↑         ↑
   ☐        ☐         ☐

1 mark

**16** The verb in the sentence below should be in the **present progressive**. Circle **one** word that needs to be changed.

The children were doing a science experiment with wires, batteries and electric lamps.

1 mark

**17** Complete the sentence below with a word formed from the root word <u>phone</u>.

The pop star sang into a _____ so everyone could hear her at the concert.

1 mark

**18** Tick **one** box in each row to show whether each sentence is in the **present progressive** or the **present perfect**.

| Sentence | Present progressive | Present perfect |
|---|---|---|
| The children are playing in the playground. | | |
| Donal has finished his reading book. | | |
| I am walking to school. | | |

2 marks

| 19 | Circle the correct word to show that there is more than one sister. |

My  sisters' / sister's  favourite drink is milkshake.

*1 mark*

| 20 | Which word is a **synonym** of the word <u>cool</u>? |

Tick **one**.

rainy ☐

windy ☐

warm ☐

chilly ☐

*1 mark*

| 21 | Write the correct word in the box to complete the sentence below. |

were        are        is

Jamie [         ] playing football with Sasha.

*1 mark*

| 22 | Tick **one** box in each row to show whether the sentence uses the **present progressive** tense. |

| Sentence | Yes | No |
| --- | --- | --- |
| Zara is baking some cakes for her friends. | | |
| Ali's eating the cakes. | | |
| Sasha didn't want any cakes. | | |

*2 marks*

**23** Complete the sentence below with a word formed from the root word help.

Mrs Jones says the children in our class are really _____ because we all tidy the classroom and put things away.

1 mark

**24** Which underlined group of words is a **fronted adverbial**?

Tick **one**.

If I tidy my room, I'll get my pocket money. ☐

One day last week, we went to town. ☐

Tammy and Gina bought some comics. ☐

Because I won the race, I was awarded a gold medal. ☐

1 mark

**25** Complete the sentence with one of the options below so that it is in the **present perfect** tense.

ate    had eaten    was eaten    has eaten

Jamal [          ] the whole packet of biscuits!

1 mark

**26** Tick the option that shows how the underlined words in the sentence below are used.

Sooner than expected, the coach arrived at the outdoor adventure centre.

Tick **one**.

- as a fronted adverbial ☐
- as a noun phrase ☐
- as a subordinate clause ☐
- as a main clause ☐

1 mark

**27** Replace the underlined word or words in each sentence with the correct **pronoun**.

When Pavel got his new bike, Pavel was excited.

[ ]

The bike was blue and the bike had big shiny wheels.

[ ]

1 mark

**28** Replace the underlined word in each sentence with the correct **possessive pronoun**.

That ball belongs to him. That ball is _____.

This jigsaw belongs to her. This jigsaw is _____.

The pizza is for both of them. The pizza is _____.

1 mark

**29** Insert a **semi-colon** in the correct place in the sentence below.

Come and see me later I do not have time to see you now.

1 mark

**30** What is the grammatical term for the underlined word?

Some trees, such as pine trees, keep their leaves all year round. Others, such as oak trees, lose their leaves in the autumn.

Tick **one**.

noun ☐
pronoun ☐
verb ☐
adverb ☐

1 mark

**31** Circle the **possessive pronoun** in the sentence below.

"This pencil's broken. Can I borrow one of yours?" asked Jimmy.

1 mark

**32** Use an **apostrophe** to write the missing word in the box.

The books belonging to the boys.

The [　　　　　　　] books.

1 mark

**33** Tick **one** box to show the correct place for a **colon** in the sentence below.

Tick **one**.

Theo needed to think carefully about the maths test it looked hard.

1 mark

**34** Insert a **hyphen** in the correct place in the sentence below.

I have a collection of well known traditional tales on my bookshelf.

1 mark

**35** Which option completes the sentence in the **present perfect**?

Sophie _____ her reading book so she's going to choose a new one.

Tick **one**.

had finished ☐

finished ☐

have finished ☐

has finished ☐

1 mark

**36** Tick the sentence that shows Sam has some toys he doesn't use very often.

Tick **one**.

Sam has some little-used toys in his cupboard. ☐

Sam has some little used toys in his cupboard. ☐

1 mark

**37** Circle the correct underlined word so that the sentence uses the **subjunctive form**.

If I was / were a spaceman, I could travel to the moon.

1 mark

**38** Which option uses a **colon** to introduce a list correctly?

Tick **one**.

The children like these: games Ludo, chess and cards. ☐

The children: like these games, Ludo, chess and cards. ☐

The children like: these games Ludo, chess and cards. ☐

The children like these games: Ludo, chess and cards. ☐

1 mark

**39** Tick one box in each row to show whether the sentence uses the **subjunctive** correctly.

| Sentence | Correct | Incorrect |
| --- | --- | --- |
| I wish I was going to the cinema at the weekend. | | |
| It is important that the class sit down. | | |
| If I were older, I'd like to join the police force. | | |

2 marks

**40** Tick the sentence that shows the soldiers guarding the queen were six foot tall.

Tick **one**.

Six foot soldiers guarded the queen. ☐

Six-foot soldiers guarded the queen. ☐

1 mark

**41** Insert a **hyphen** in the correct place in the sentence below.

Zoe is a well liked member of Class 6.

1 mark

**42** Write the correct word in the box so the sentence uses the **subjunctive form**.

I'd go to town without my parents if I [ ] allowed.

1 mark

**43** Circle the two words that are **synonyms** in the passage below.

Morning lessons take place from 9 o'clock until noon. After midday, we take a break for lunch and continue our lessons until 3 o'clock.

1 mark

**44** Circle the correct underlined word so that the sentence uses the **subjunctive form**.

I wish I were / was an explorer, then I'd go to the North Pole.

1 mark

**45** Insert a **colon and** two **semi-colons** in the correct places in the sentence below.

Children need to bring the following on the school trip a waterproof coat sensible walking shoes and their pencils.

1 mark

**46** Explain how the position of the **apostrophe** changes the meaning of the second sentence.

1) My big sisters' favourite food is fruit salad.
2) My big sister's favourite food is fruit salad.

_____

_____

1 mark

Total: _____ /50

# Spring Half Term 1

**1** Add two **full stops** in the correct places below.

The spider scuttled across the floor I could see it beneath the sofa

*1 mark*

**2** Tick **all** the sentences that contain a **preposition**.

The yellow car is behind the red bus. ☐

Amina collected her book and left. ☐

Henry's house is opposite the shops. ☐

The school is beside the park. ☐

*2 marks*

**3** Add **inverted commas** to the sentence below to show what Suki is saying.

Suki shouted, Quick! Look at the baby bird.

*1 mark*

**4** Write the correct punctuation mark in the box.

Earlier this morning Joe and I played on the climbing frame.

*1 mark*

**5** Which **one prefix** can be added to all three words below to make their **antonyms**?
Write the prefix in the box.

credible

correct

accurate

[ ]

1 mark

**6** Which option is punctuated correctly?

Tick **one**.

Joe opened his lunchbox. He took out a sandwich and ate it. [ ]

Joe opened his lunchbox he took out a sandwich and ate it. [ ]

joe opened his lunchbox. he took out a sandwich and ate it. [ ]

Joe opened his lunchbox. He took out a sandwich and ate it [ ]

1 mark

**7** Tick to show whether each sentence is in the **past progressive** or **present progressive**.

| Sentence | Past progressive | Present progressive |
| --- | --- | --- |
| The dog is chasing a stick. | | |
| The cat was sleeping on a chair. | | |
| The bird was resting on a branch. | | |

2 marks

**8** Tick the **adverb of possibility** in the sentence below.

Tick **one**.

Zoe certainly should win the race – she's such as fast runner.

1 mark

**9** Punctuate this correctly to form **two** complete sentences.

the cat slept in the armchair it was curled up in a ball

_____

1 mark

**10** Insert a **semi-colon** in the correct place in the sentence below.

It's snowing I'm so excited!

1 mark

**11** Which sentence contains a **verb** in the **past progressive**?

Tick **one**.

Angus is drawing in his sketch book. ☐

Angus was drawing in his sketch book. ☐

Angus drew in his sketch book. ☐

Angus will draw in his sketch book. ☐

1 mark

**12** Explain why the underlined words start with a **capital letter**.

James Arnold is leaving Oldtown Primary School this July.

_____

_____

1 mark

**13** Insert a **pair of commas** in the correct place in the sentence below.

Anna a girl in our class is from Poland.

1 mark

**14** Rewrite the sentence below in the **past progressive** tense.

Mrs Chan walked to school this morning.

_____

1 mark

**15** Which sentence is the most **formal**?

Tick **one**.

| | |
|---|---|
| The children made an incredible discovery today. | ☐ |
| The children found out some interesting things today. | ☐ |
| Today, the kids found out some new stuff. | ☐ |
| Interesting stuff was found out by the children today. | ☐ |

1 mark

**16** Insert a **pair of brackets** in the correct place in the sentence below.

Mr Jones (our teacher) is really funny.

*1 mark*

**17** Which **tense** is used in the sentence below?

I was watching a film on my computer last night.

Tick **one**.

- simple past ☐
- simple present ☐
- past progressive ☑
- present progressive ☐

*1 mark*

**18** Circle the **two** words that are **synonyms** in the passage below.

Grandpa loves his garden but he hates weeds. Sometimes he (kills) the weeds by pulling them out. Other times he (destroys) them with poison.

*1 mark*

**19** Tick to show where the **inverted commas** should go in the sentence below.

Tick **two**.

Toby said, ✓Can I have that comic after you?✓

*1 mark*

**20** What is the grammatical term for the underlined words in the sentence below?

As it was a hot day, we drank <u>fresh lemonade with ice cubes</u>.

Tick **one**.

| | |
|---|---|
| an exclamation | ☐ |
| a main clause | ☐ |
| an expanded noun phrase | ☐ |
| a command | ☐ |

1 mark

**21** Write the name of punctuation that could be used instead of **brackets** in the sentence below.

Miss Hamer (a teacher at our school) works in Year 2.

_____

1 mark

**22** Rewrite the sentence below as **direct speech**. Remember to punctuate your sentence correctly.

I said I wanted to take the shortcut.

I said, _____

1 mark

**23** Complete the sentence with a **preposition phrase**

The choir of children sang _____.

1 mark

**24** Insert a **comma** in the correct place in the sentence below.

Once we got home we had a drink of juice and a biscuit.

1 mark

**25** Complete the sentence by adding a **fronted adverbial**.

_____ Dan and Rachel made jam sandwiches.

1 mark

**26** Insert a **colon** in the correct place in the sentence below.

There are two places that I have always wanted to visit New York and Paris.

1 mark

**27** Use **parenthesis** to punctuate the sentence below.

Sophie's mum who is our school cook bakes the best cookies ever.

1 mark

**28** Complete the sentence below with an **adverb of possibility**.

Our class are _____ going to win on Sports Day because we've got all the best athletes in the school.

1 mark

**29** Tick **one** box in each row to show whether the sentence is written in the **active** or the **passive.**

| Sentence | Active | Passive |
| --- | --- | --- |
| Everyone played on the field. | | |
| The bread was baked by the baker. | | |
| The whistle was blown by Mr Gee. | | |

2 marks

Year 6: Spring Half Term Test 1

**30** Circle the **adverb** that shows you are most sure you will be chosen to take part in the school play.

I will possibly / certainly be chosen to take part in the school play.

1 mark

**31** Insert a **comma** in the correct place in the sentence below.

After a long day at school I lay on my bed and read my book.

1 mark

**32** Which **one prefix** can be added to all three words below to make their **antonyms**?
Write the prefix in the box.

interested
impressed
happy

1 mark

**33** Write the correct punctuation mark in the box.

I have two best friends Jamie and Joseph.

1 mark

**34** Rewrite the sentence below in the **passive voice**.
Remember to punctuate your sentence correctly.

The children chased the football.

1 mark

**35** Which sentence is the most **formal**?

Tick **one**.

Don't go spending too much time on your computer! ☐

Spending too much time on a computer should be avoided. ☐

Lots of computer time isn't all that good for you. ☐

You're mad if you spend too much time on a computer. ☐

1 mark

**36** Tick the option that shows how the underlined words are used in the sentence.

The newspaper shop <u>across the road</u> is where my mum works.

Tick **one**.

as a main clause ☐

as a relative clause ☐

as a preposition phrase ☐

as a fronted adverbial ☐

1 mark

**37** Insert a **semi-colon** in the correct place in the sentence below.

Anita was a great rugby player she scored lots of points.

1 mark

**38** Which punctuation mark should be used in the place indicated by the arrow?

Gus is excellent at sport ↑ he plays cricket and football.

Tick **one**.

comma ☐

hyphen ☐

full stop ☐

semi-colon ☐

1 mark

**39** Circle the most **formal** option in each box below to complete the invitation.

You are | asked / invited / told | to attend a meeting

where we will | inform / tell / update | you about your child's progress.

The meeting will | start / begin / commence | at 5 o'clock.

2 marks

**40** Tick **one** box in each row to show whether the sentence is written in the **active** or the **passive**.

| Sentence | Active | Passive |
| --- | --- | --- |
| Everyone played chase. | | |
| The book was read by the teacher. | | |
| The parcel was delivered by the post lady. | | |

2 marks

**41** Write the correct **adverb of possibility** in the box to complete the sentence below.

clearly          possibly          perhaps

It's [_____] a good idea to practise before a times tables test if you want to do your best.

1 mark

**42** Rewrite the sentence below as **direct speech**. Remember to punctuate your sentence correctly.

Mr Smith told us to put on our coats.

Mr Smith said, _____

1 mark

**43** Circle the **two** words that are **antonyms** in the sentence below.

I emptied my cupboard, making a pile of worthless old toys and another pile of my most valuable treasures.

1 mark

**44** Write the sentence below in the **active**.
Remember to punctuate your sentence correctly.

The window was broken by the children.

_____

1 mark

**45** Create a **bullet-pointed list** for these ingredients: bread, butter and cheese.
Remember to punctuate your answer correctly.

To make cheese on toast, you will need these ingredients:

1 mark

Total: _____ /50

Year 6: Spring Half Term Test 2

| Name: | Year: | Date: |

# Spring Half Term 2

**1** Circle all the **determiners** in the sentence below.

Behind the sofa, I found a pound coin, an unwrapped toffee and a blue felt-tipped pen.

1 mark

**2** Tick to show where a **comma** should go in the sentence below.

Tick **one**.

Abi's sweets had red yellow and purple coloured wrappers.

1 mark

**3** Add **inverted commas** to the sentence below to show what Seema is saying.

Seema announced, I would like to be a doctor when I grow up.

1 mark

**4** Write the correct word in the box in the sentence below.

usable     useful     misuse

A calculator is really [    ] when you're solving maths problems.

1 mark

**5** Tick **one** box in each row to show whether the sentence is in the **present progressive** or the **present perfect**.

| Sentence | Present progressive | Present perfect |
|---|---|---|
| The twins have bathed the dog. | | |
| Joe has finished his homework. | | |
| Aliyah is walking to school. | | |

2 marks

**6** Circle the correct word to show that there is only one school.

The school's / schools' teachers went to a meeting.

1 mark

**7** What is the grammatical term for the underlined words?

<u>Quickly and quietly</u>, the mouse scurried across the floor.

Tick **one**.

a main clause ☐

a noun phrase ☐

a subordinate clause ☐

a fronted adverbial ☐

1 mark

**8** Choose the correct word to complete each sentence.
Write the word on the line.

There was _____ bunch of bananas in the fruit bowl.

> a / an

There was also _____ enormous red apple.

> a / an

I chopped them up and made _____ fruit salad.

> a / an

1 mark

**9** Which option uses **commas** correctly?

Tick **one**.

I have pens paper, crayons and pencils. ☐

I have pens, paper crayons and pencils. ☐

I have pens, paper crayons and, pencils. ☐

I have pens, paper, crayons and pencils. ☐

1 mark

**10** What does the root word <u>aqua</u> mean in the word family below?

**aqua**tic    **aqua**marine    **aqua**rium    **aqua**lung

Tick **one**.

sky ☐

water ☐

earth ☐

fire ☐

*1 mark*

**11** Add **two commas** to the sentence below to make it clear that Carlo has four things in his pocket.

Carlo has an old bus ticket an elastic band a sweet wrapper and his front door key in his pocket.

*1 mark*

**12** Tick **one** box in each row to show whether the sentence is in the **past perfect** or the **present perfect**.

| Sentence | Past perfect | Present perfect |
| --- | --- | --- |
| The children have eaten their lunch. | | |
| Martin has finished his drawing. | | |
| I had tried my best in the test. | | |

*2 marks*

**13** Insert a **colon** in the correct place in the sentence below.

There are two things that I have always wanted a camera and a telescope.

1 mark

**14** Underline the **adverbial** in the sentence below.

In the summer holidays, I'm going to a Scout camp.

1 mark

**15** Tick to show where the **colon** should go in the sentence below.

Tick **one**.

It is a big school there are 15 classes.
  ☐              ☐              ☐

1 mark

**16** Which sentence is in **Standard English**?

Tick **one**.

I went to the cinema with my sister.   ☐

I been to school today.   ☐

We seen a peacock at the zoo.   ☐

I already done my reading today.   ☐

1 mark

**17** Which **one prefix** can be added to all three words below to make their **antonyms**?
Write the prefix in the box.

believable

acceptable

reasonable

[ ]

1 mark

**18** Circle the correct **verb form** in each underlined pair to complete the sentences below.

Gus is / are reading a book in the book corner.

In our school, there is / are lots of kind teachers.

My granny thinks it is / are a good film.

1 mark

**19** Rewrite the sentence so that the **reporting clause** comes after the **direct speech**.

Miss Lane whispered, "It's important to be quiet in the library."

_____

1 mark

**20** Underline the **relative clause** in the sentence below.

I have a brilliant bike that is shiny and blue.

1 mark

**21** Write a **modal verb** in the box to complete the sentence below.

In our class, you put your hand up if you [ ] answer a question.

*1 mark*

**22** Rewrite the sentence below so that it has a **fronted adverbial**.

Our postman has already delivered our post by the time the sun comes up.

_____

*1 mark*

**23** Circle the correct underlined word so that the sentence uses the **subjunctive form**.

I wish I was / were able to come to the party, but sadly I'm unavailable.

*1 mark*

**24** Tick **one** box in each row to show whether the underlined noun is **singular** or **plural**.

| Sentence | Singular | Plural |
|---|---|---|
| The girls' books were kept on a shelf. | | |
| The princess's shoes were covered in mud. | | |
| The boys' football boots were left by the door. | | |

*2 marks*

**25** Rewrite the sentence below with the correct punctuation.

would you like to come to my party Asked Sophie

_____

1 mark

**26** Which option correctly completes the sentence below?

Mr Zain pointed at the pile of coats on the cloakroom floor and asked, "_____ are these? Please get them tidied up."

Tick **one**.

| | |
|---|---|
| Whom | ☐ |
| Whose | ☐ |
| Who | ☐ |
| Who's | ☐ |

1 mark

**27** Tick to show where the **omitted relative pronoun** should go.

Tick **one**.

The kitten Zoe was stroking was extremely cute and fluffy.
　　　↑　　　　　↑　　　　　↑
　　　☐　　　　　☐　　　　　☐

1 mark

**28** Complete the sentence below with a **modal verb** to show uncertainty.

I haven't been very well so I _____ not be allowed to play out with my friends.

1 mark

Year 6: Spring Half Term Test 2

**29** Tick the sentence that uses a **colon** to introduce a list correctly.

Tick **one**.

These are my favourite animals mice: snakes, and spiders. ☐

These are my favourite animals: mice, snakes and spiders. ☐

These are my: favourite animals mice, snakes and spiders. ☐

These: are my favourite animals mice, snakes and spiders. ☐

1 mark

**30** Circle the **modal verbs** in the sentences below.

I should do my homework.

Emily can count to ten in French.

We might go to the park after school.

1 mark

**31** Insert a **comma** in the correct place in the sentence below to show that two children went to the theatre.

After leaving Jimmy Jo and Fergal went to the theatre.

1 mark

**32** Tick the sentence that uses a **dash** correctly.

Tick **one**.

Our class – can get quite noisy there are so many children. ☐

Our class can get quite noisy there are so many – children. ☐

Our class can get quite noisy – there are so many children. ☐

Our class can get quite noisy there are – so many children. ☐

1 mark

**33** Tick to show where the **semi-colon** should go in the sentence below.

Tick **one**.

The trip was brilliant I had a great time.
        □              □         □

1 mark

**34** Tick **one** box in each row to show whether the **hyphen** has been used correctly or incorrectly.

| Sentence | Correct | Incorrect |
|---|---|---|
| The bad-tempered child was misbehaving. | | |
| The footpath was dog-friendly. | | |
| The ice-cream-cone was toffee flavoured. | | |

2 marks

**35** Rewrite the sentence below in the **active**.
Remember to punctuate your sentence correctly.

The whistle was blown by the teacher.

_____

1 mark

**36** Insert **one hyphen** and **one comma** in the correct places in the sentence below.

My sister is an ice skating champion a swimmer and a runner.

1 mark

**37** Tick **one** box in each row to show whether the **subjunctive** has been formed correctly or incorrectly.

| Sentence | Correct | Incorrect |
| --- | --- | --- |
| I wish I were able to do a cartwheel. | | |
| If I were able, I'd like to compete in the Olympics. | | |
| I wish I was going to the circus tonight. | | |

2 marks

**38** Explain how the position of the **apostrophe** changes the meaning of the second sentence.

1) My baby sister's room is painted yellow.
2) My baby sisters' room is painted yellow.

_____

_____

1 mark

**39** Insert **one colon and two semi-colons** in the correct places in the sentence below.

At the safari park, you can see groups of children families of monkeys and a pride of lions.

1 mark

**40** Which word is an **antonym** of the verb <u>conclude</u>?

Tick **one**.

end ☐

begin ☐

theory ☐

finish ☐

1 mark

**41** Tick **one** box in each row to show whether the sentence is written in the **active** or **passive**.

| Sentence | Active | Passive |
|---|---|---|
| The alien was found by the children. | | |
| Everyone watched the film. | | |
| Yoko was doing a painting. | | |

2 marks

**42** Insert a **comma** and a **dash** in the correct places in the sentence below.

This weekend I am going to get a dog the first I've ever owned.

1 mark

**43** Explain how the use of **commas** changes the meaning of the two sentences.

1) Most of the time, travellers are worried about getting lost.

2) Most of the time travellers are worried about getting lost.

_____

_____

1 mark

**44** Write a sentence in the **passive**.

_____

_____

1 mark

Total: _____ /50

# Summer Half Term 1

**1** Circle each word that should begin with a **capital letter** in the sentence below.

These are the people in the library club: logan, sasha, victor and amy.

1 mark

**2** Tick **one** box to show where a **comma** should go in the sentence below.

Tick **one**.

I go to netball practice every Tuesday Thursday and Saturday.

1 mark

**3** Circle all the **determiners** in the sentence below.

In the book corner, we've got a shelf of picture books, a collection of fiction books and an old box of atlases.

1 mark

**4** Tick the **subordinating conjunction** in the sentence below.

Tick **one**.

Dad said I can go to the park when I have finished my homework.

1 mark

Year 6: Summer Half Term Test 1

**5** Draw a line to match each group of words to its contraction.

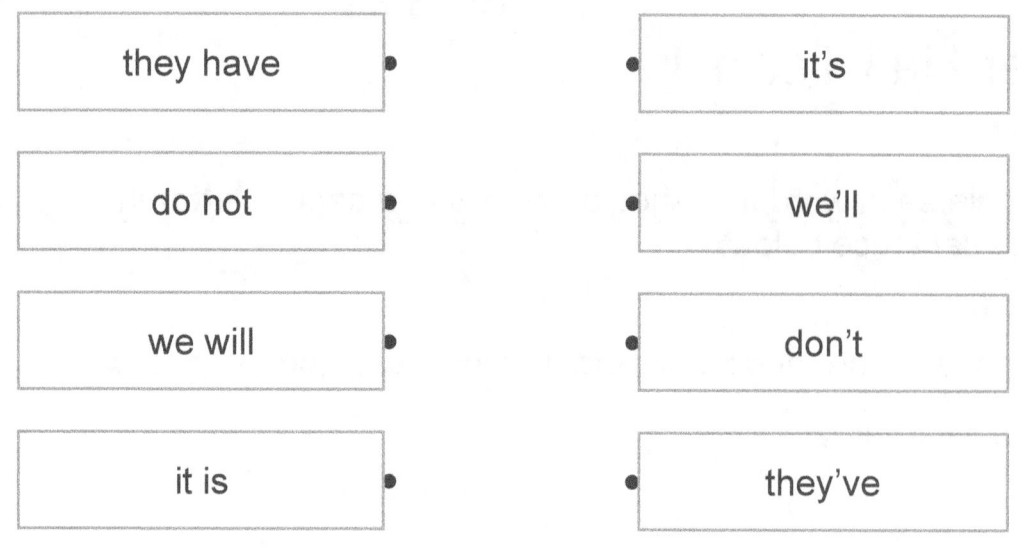

1 mark

**6** Circle each word that should begin with a **capital letter** in the sentence below.

I am going to the zoo with eva and hanna at the weekend.

1 mark

**7** The sentence below should be in the **present progressive** tense. Circle **one** word that needs to be changed.

Sasha was completing a jigsaw with her little brother.

1 mark

**8** Add **two commas** to the sentence below to make it clear that Olga has four things in her pencil case.

Olga has a pencil a pen some coloured crayons and a ruler in her pencil case.

1 mark

**9** Replace the underlined words in the sentences below with their expanded forms.

Let's go outside and play football, I'll go and get my ball.

[ ]          [ ]

We can ask Dan and Izzy if they'd like to play too.

[ ]

1 mark

**10** Which word class is the underlined word in the sentence below?

We had some tasty soup for our lunch today.

Tick **one**.

noun [ ]

adverb [ ]

verb [ ]

adjective [ ]

1 mark

**11** Circle the word in the passage that contains an **apostrophe** for **omission**.

Ravi's mum asked if I'd like to go for tea at their house.
I asked my mum and she said I could go.

1 mark

**12** Tick the **preposition** in the sentence below.

Tick **one**.

The children had playtime after assembly.
⇧ ⇧ ⇧
☐ ☐ ☐

1 mark

**13** Complete the sentence below by writing the **conjunctions** from the box in the correct places. Use each conjunction only once.

| but | and | or |

For dinner you can have either fish _____ chips _____ pizza and chips, _____ you can't have pudding unless you finish your first course.

1 mark

**14** Which option completes the sentence in the **present progressive**?

Harry _____ football with his friends.

Tick **one**.

played ☐

has played ☐

is playing ☐

was playing ☐

1 mark

**15** Write the correct word in the box to complete the sentence below.

therefore     while     so     before

Dad does the ironing [          ] he takes us to school.

1 mark

**16** Draw a line to match each sentence to the correct **determiner**.
Use each determiner only once.

| Sentence | Determiner |
|---|---|
| Mum bought me _____ ice cream. | the |
| It had _____ chocolate flake in the top. | an |
| _____ cone was toffee flavoured. | a |

1 mark

**17** Rewrite the sentence below in the **present progressive**.

Mr Hooper teaches the children how to multiply decimal fractions.

_____

1 mark

**18** Choose the correct word to complete each sentence. Write the word on the line.

I saw _____ boy playing on the swings.

[ a / an ]

He was eating _____ orange.

[ a / an ]

I went and played with him for _____ while.

[ a / an ]

1 mark

**19** Which one **prefix** can be added to all three words below to make new words?
Write the prefix in the box.

_____school

_____cook

_____mature

[            ]

1 mark

**20** Write the words <u>could not</u> as one word, using an **apostrophe**.

I _____ open the jar of jam so I asked my dad to do it for me.

1 mark

**21** Which **one prefix** can be added to all three words below to make new words?
Write the prefix in the box.

_____social

_____septic

_____clockwise

1 mark

**22** Draw a line to match each **prefix** to a word to make **four** different words.
Use each prefix only once.

pre — marine

sub — historic

auto — sonic

super — biography

1 mark

**23** Write a **preposition** in the box to complete the sentence below.

I found my pencil [        ] my bag.

1 mark

**24** Tick the correct word to complete the sentence below.

There is a flag flying _____ the top of the flagpole.

Tick **one**.

under ☐

in ☐

at ☐

down ☐

1 mark

**25** Tick **one** box in each row to show whether the sentence is written in the **simple past** or the **past progressive**.

| Sentence | Simple past | Past progressive |
| --- | --- | --- |
| Ravi was doing a handstand. | | |
| Lucy skipped in the playground. | | |
| Hamid was doing a puzzle. | | |

2 marks

**26** Rewrite the sentence below so that it has a **fronted adverbial**.

Class 6 will be performing their play to the school next week.

_____

1 mark

**27** Tick **one** box in each row to show whether the underlined word is an **adjective** or an **adverb**.

| Sentence | Adjective | Adverb |
|---|---|---|
| Gus had a shiny bike. | | |
| The bike had big wheels. | | |
| Gus rode the bike quickly. | | |

2 marks

**28** Tick **all** the sentences that contain a **preposition**.

Maisie is below Jas on the climbing frame. ☐

Eva is sliding down the slide. ☐

Ben is whizzing around on the roundabout. ☐

Mrs Baines is watching the children play. ☐

2 marks

**29** Write a suitable **adjective** to complete the **noun phrase**.

At the pet shop there are lots of _____ animals.

1 mark

**30** Tick **one** box in each row to show whether the sentence is written in the **active** or the **passive**.

| Sentence | Active | Passive |
|---|---|---|
| The teacher read the story. | | |
| The cake was made by the baker. | | |
| Nina was watching a film. | | |

2 marks

**31** Rewrite the sentence below so that it has a **fronted adverbial**.

Ravi and Joshi went to the park with their aunty after school.

_____

1 mark

**32** The **prefix** dis- can be added to the root word connect to make the word **disconnect**.
What does the word **disconnect** mean?

Tick **one**.

join together ☐

take apart ☐

cut up ☐

meet up ☐

1 mark

**33** Which sentence is the most **formal**?

Tick **one**.

It's important to be punctual. ☐

Don't you dare be late! ☐

If you're late, we'll go without you. ☐

You'll need to get a move on! ☐

1 mark

**34** Draw a line to match each **prefix** to a word to make **four** different words.
Use each prefix only once.

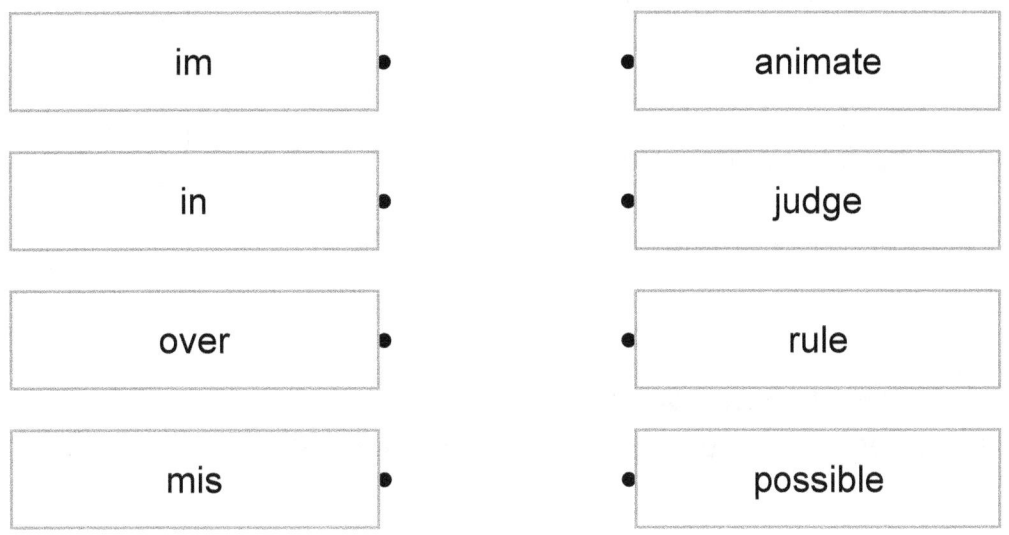

1 mark

**35** Write the correct word in the box in the sentence below.

mismatched    mismanaged    misfortune

Sammi made a dinner of tinned fish covered in banana custard.
It was a [ ] combination of foods.

1 mark

**36** Insert a **semi-colon** in the correct place in the sentence below.

I'll play with you tomorrow I have to go to my gran's house right now.

1 mark

**37** Which sentence is the most **formal**?

Tick **one**.

If you don't use the front door, you'll get told off. ☐

Use the front door, thanks. ☐

Only use the front door, or else! ☐

Please enter the school by the front entrance. ☐

1 mark

**38** Rewrite the sentence below in the **active**.
Remember to punctuate your answer correctly.

The machine was repaired by the engineer.

_____

1 mark

**39** Which **one prefix** can be added to all three words below to make their **antonyms**?
Write the prefix in the box.

code

clutter

mist

☐

1 mark

**40** Which sentence uses a **colon** to introduce a list correctly?

Tick **one**.

I like these fruits: apples, oranges and pears. ☐

I like: these fruits apples, oranges, and pears. ☐

I like these fruits, apples: oranges and pears. ☐

I like these: fruits, apples, oranges and pears. ☐

1 mark

**41** Rewrite the sentence below in the **passive.**
Remember to punctuate your answer correctly.

The teacher read the book.

_____

1 mark

**42** Insert a **colon** in the correct place in the sentence below.

My favourite colour is red it is the colour of my favourite football team.

1 mark

**43** Which verb is a **synonym** of the verb <u>sigh</u>?

Tick **one**.

hail ☐

wail ☐

exhale ☐

inhale ☐

1 mark

**44** Insert a **dash** in the correct place in the sentence below.

All the children wore the same blue blazers and stripy ties.

1 mark

**45** Circle the **two** words that are **synonyms** in the passage below.

During the New Year sales, many shops slash their prices. Cutting prices in this way encourages shoppers to spend more money.

1 mark

**46** Which one **prefix** can be added to all three words below to make their **antonyms**?
Write the prefix in the box.

honest

obey

advantage

[ ]

1 mark

Total: _____ /50

# Summer Half Term 2

**1** Circle each word that should begin with a **capital letter** in the sentence below.

jamal went on a trip to london. He saw buckingham palace and trafalgar square, and rode on an open-top red bus.

1 mark

**2** Circle the **conjunction** in the sentence below.

I love Fridays because we go swimming.

1 mark

**3** Why do the underlined words in the sentence below start with a **capital letter**?

Next <u>September</u>, <u>Mrs Clarke</u> is going to be a teacher at <u>Redroof Primary School</u>.

_____

_____

1 mark

**4** Write an **apostrophe** in the correct place in the sentence below.

I have borrowed Donals football.

1 mark

**5** Write the correct word in the box in the sentence below.

misbehave    behaved    behaviour

Class 6R won an award in assembly because of their excellent ☐.

1 mark

**6** Which option is punctuated correctly?

Tick **one**.

I waited at the bus stop eventually. The bus came and I got on. ☐

I waited at the bus stop eventually the bus came and I got on. ☐

I waited at the bus stop. Eventually, the bus came and I got on. ☐

I waited at the bus stop. eventually the bus came and I got on ☐

1 mark

**7** Rewrite the sentence below in the **past progressive**.

James and David played football at the weekend.

_____

1 mark

**8** Circle the word in the passage below that contains an **apostrophe** for **possession**.

Netball is Seema's favourite game but it isn't mine. I'd rather play hockey.

1 mark

**9** Tick the correct word to complete the sentence below.

I fell off the climbing frame and bumped my head _____ Mum took me to the hospital.

Tick **one**.

therefore ☐

so ☐

next ☐

since ☐

1 mark

**10** Which **tense** is used in the sentence below?

Zara and Milly were eating pizza at the new restaurant in town.

Tick **one**.

simple past ☐

simple present ☐

past progressive ☐

present progressive ☐

1 mark

**11** What does the root word <u>chron</u> mean in the word family below?

chronology    chronicle    synchronise    chronological

Tick **one**.

metal ☐

together ☐

order ☐

time ☐

*1 mark*

**12** Tick **one** box in each row to show whether each sentence is in the **present perfect** or the **past perfect**.

| Sentence | Present perfect | Past perfect |
|---|---|---|
| Jo had played outside all afternoon. | | |
| I have walked ten miles for charity. | | |
| The dog has eaten my homework! | | |

*2 marks*

**13** What is the grammatical term for the underlined words?

<u>The friendly teacher with ginger hair</u> takes us for PE.

_____

*1 mark*

**14** Circle the correct word to complete the sentence below.

The <u>boy's</u> / <u>boys</u> toys were left all over the floor.

*1 mark*

**15.** Add **inverted commas** to the sentence below to show what Sam is saying.

Sam shouted, Pass the ball! Pass the ball, quick!

*1 mark*

**16.** Rewrite the sentence below in **Standard English**.

We was looking forward to our trip to the zoo.

_____

*1 mark*

**17.** Complete the sentence below with a **noun phrase** formed with a **preposition**.

The squirrel climbed a tree _____.

*1 mark*

**18.** Replace the underlined word or words in each sentence with the correct **possessive pronoun**.

That dog belongs to <u>them</u>. That dog is _____.

This brush belongs to <u>my sister</u>. This brush is _____.

The parcel is for <u>you</u>. The parcel is _____.

*1 mark*

**19** Rewrite the sentence below as **direct speech**.
Remember to punctuate your sentence correctly.

Bryn said that he is going to watch United play City at the weekend.

_____

_____

1 mark

**20** Circle the correct word to show that there is more than one neighbour.

Our neighbours' / neighbour's cats like to sleep in our garden.

1 mark

**21** What is the grammatical term for the underlined word?

Some animals, such as dormice, hibernate during the winter. Others, such as squirrels, remain awake but stay in their homes on particularly cold days.

Tick **one**.

noun ☐

pronoun ☐

verb ☐

adverb ☐

1 mark

**22** Which one **suffix** can be added to all three words below to make **adjectives**?
Write the suffix on the line.

consider
affection
passion

_____

1 mark

**23** Tick one box to show where a **comma** should go in the sentence below.

Tick **one**.

In the future people may no longer use cars to travel.

☐ ☐ ☐ ☐

1 mark

**24** Circle the correct **relative pronoun** in the sentence below.

We have a dog that / what likes long walks in the park.

1 mark

**25** Complete the sentence below with a **modal verb** to show uncertainty.

If you go out to play in the winter without a coat you _____ feel cold.

1 mark

**26** Write a sentence that includes a **fronted adverbial**.

_____

_____

1 mark

**27** a) Draw a line to match each **noun** to a **suffix** to make **three** verbs.

| hospital |   | ate |
| captive  |   | ify |
| intense  |   | ise |

1 mark

b) Write the words on the line below.

_____

1 mark

**28** Explain how the **apostrophe** changes the meaning of the second sentence.

1) There was long green grass in the cows' field.
2) There was long green grass in the cow's field.

_____

_____

1 mark

**29** Underline the **relative clause** in the sentence below.

I have a jacket that is white and black.

1 mark

**30** Circle the **adverb of possibility** in the sentence below.

Perhaps Granny will bring us a present when she comes back from her holiday.

1 mark

**31** Use **parenthesis** to punctuate the sentence below.

While walking to school, James Arnold a pupil from St Mary's Primary rescued a kitten from a tree.

1 mark

**32** Explain how the **modal verb** changes the meaning of the second sentence.

1) Class 6B will be going to the zoo next week.
2) Class 6B might be going to the zoo next week.

_____

_____

1 mark

**33** Tick **one** box in each row to show whether the sentence is written in the **active** or the **passive**.

| Sentence | Active | Passive |
|---|---|---|
| The chair was broken. | | |
| The dog was walked by its owner. | | |
| The cat was sleeping. | | |

2 marks

**34** Tick the sentence that shows the child is asking to paint Miss Sohal.

Tick **one**.

"May I paint Miss Sohal?" asked Jimmy. ☐

"May I paint, Miss Sohal?" asked Jimmy. ☐

1 mark

**35** Which **verb** completes the sentence so that it uses the **subjunctive form**?

If I _____ you, I'd save that cake for later.

Tick **one**.

be ☐

was ☐

am ☐

were ☐

1 mark

**36** Circle the correct underlined word so that the sentence uses the **subjunctive form**.

If I were / was a millionaire, I'd buy a fast racing car.

1 mark

**37** Tick the sentence that uses a **dash** correctly.

Tick **one**.

I really struggle with maths – it's just so confusing. ☐

I really struggle – with maths it's just so confusing. ☐

I really struggle with maths it's just so – confusing. ☐

I really – struggle with maths it's just so confusing. ☐

1 mark

**38** a) Write an explanation of the word **antonym**.

_____

_____

1 mark

b) Write one word that is an **antonym** of calm.

_____

1 mark

**39** Insert a **hyphen** in the correct place in the sentence below.

My parents like the restaurant because it has a child friendly atmosphere.

1 mark

**40** Rewrite the sentence below in the **active**.
Remember to punctuate your answer correctly.

The toys were put away by the children.

_____

1 mark

**41** Insert a **semi-colon** in the correct place in the sentence below.

I have a new bag it has red spots and a green strap.

1 mark

**42** Which sentence is the most **formal**?

Tick **one**.

We request that pupils wear school uniform at all times. ☐

You'll be in big trouble if you don't wear your uniform. ☐

Can you wear your uniform, please? ☐

Come in your uniform every day. ☐

1 mark

**43** Insert a **colon** and **two semi-colons** in the correct places in the sentence below.

On her desk, Mrs Cooper has the following items a stapler a pot of pencils and an apple.

1 mark

Year 6: Summer Half Term Test 2

**44** Create a **bullet-pointed list** for these ingredients: milk, ice-cream and strawberries.
Remember to punctuate your answer correctly.

To make a milkshake, you will need these ingredients:

1 mark

**45** Explain how the **hyphen** changes the meaning of the second sentence.

1) There are five metre ropes in the school hall.

2) There are five-metre ropes in the school hall.

_____

_____

1 mark

**46** Write a sentence using the **subjunctive**.
Remember to use correct punctuation.

1 mark

Total: _____ /50

Year 6: Autumn Half Term Test 1 – Mark scheme

# Mark scheme for Autumn Half Term 1

| Qu. | Requirement | Mark |
|---|---|---|
| 1<br>G5 | **Award 1 mark** for *sophie*, *lottie*, *amal* and *jo* circled. | 1m |
| 2<br>G3 | **Award 1 mark** for *when* circled. | 1m |
| 3<br>G5 | **Award 2 marks** for all three boxes ticked correctly, **award 1 mark** for two boxes ticked correctly:<br>On Saturday, seema is going to Birmingham. = Incorrect<br>Cassie is going to glasgow in June. = Incorrect<br>Jamal went to Cardiff last summer. = Correct | 2m |
| 4<br>G1 | **Award 1 mark** for *the*, *an*, *a* and *a* circled. | 1m |
| 5<br>G5 | **Award 1 mark** for an apostrophe inserted before the *s* in *Browns*: Mrs Brown's dog has a loud bark. | 1m |
| 6<br>G5 | **Award 1 mark** for a tick next to the third option: "Let's play skipping at break time," said Shaz. | 1m |
| 7<br>G1 G6 | **Award 1 mark** for *accurate* and *affectionate* written on the lines. | 1m |
| 8<br>G5 | **Award 1 mark** for a question mark inserted at the end of the sentence. | 1m |
| 9<br>G5 | **Award 1 mark** for a tick next to the fourth option: apostrophe | 1m |
| 10<br>G5 | **Award 1 mark** for two full stops added correctly: It's my birthday on Friday. I am going to have a party with cake and balloons. | 1m |
| 11<br>G3 | **Award 1 mark** for *because* circled. | 1m |
| 12<br>G1 | **Award 1 mark** for *a*, *an* and *a* written on the lines. | 1m |
| 13<br>G3 | **Award 1 mark** for a tick next to the fourth option: who | 1m |
| 14<br>G5 | **Award 2 marks** for all three boxes ticked correctly, **award 1 mark** for two boxes ticked correctly:<br>Dads magazine is about car's. = Incorrect<br>I borrowed Joe's pencil. = Correct<br>Amit's mum is a nurse.= Correct | 2m |
| 15<br>G5 | **Award 1 mark** for a pair of brackets inserted correctly: The Eiffel Tower (in Paris) is 324 metres tall. | 1m |
| 16<br>G5 | **Award 2 marks** for all three boxes ticked correctly, **award 1 mark** for two boxes ticked correctly:<br>The dog's basket is in the kitchen. = Possessive<br>I practised my spellings last night. = Plural<br>The children put their books in their bags. = Plural | 2m |

# Year 6: Autumn Half Term Test 1 – Mark scheme

| Qu. | Requirement | Mark |
|---|---|---|
| 17 G5 | **Award 1 mark** for each item placed on a separate line with lowercase letters used throughout. Accept commas or semi-colons at the ends of lines 1 and 2 with a full stop after the final point. | 1m |
| 18 G1 | **Award 1 mark** for all three lines drawn correctly:<br>Sam gave me <u>a</u> sweet.<br>It was <u>the</u> tastiest sweet in the world.<br>Now I've got <u>an</u> achy tooth. | 1m |
| 19 G5 | **Award 1 mark** for a tick next to the third option: Gus went to Gran's house on Sunday. | 1m |
| 20 G5 | **Award 1 mark** for *cats* circled. | 1m |
| 21 G3 | **Award 1 mark** for *which* circled. | 1m |
| 22 G5 | **Award 1 mark** for the correct punctuation: Ali said, "I would like to play football on Saturday." | 1m |
| 23 G4 | **Award 1 mark** for *might*, *may* or *could* written on the line. | 1m |
| 24 G1 | **Award 1 mark** for a tick next to the fourth option: It will definitely stop snowing soon. | 1m |
| 25 G5 | **Award 1 mark** for *I said, "I am going to visit my granny on Sunday."* or *"I am going to visit my granny on Sunday," I said.* | 1m |
| 26 G1 G6 | **Award 1 mark** for *equalise* written on the line. | 1m |
| 27 G3 | **Award 1 mark** for *who is a police officer* underlined: | 1m |
| 28 G5 | **Award 1 mark** for a semi-colon inserted after *school*: There is a huge field near our school; it is being ploughed tomorrow. | 1m |
| 29 G4 | **Award 1 mark** for *can*, *may* and *may* circled. | 1m |
| 30 G5 | **Award 1 mark** for writing any from: *(a pair of) brackets, (a pair of) dashes*. | 1m |
| 31 G7 | **Award 1 mark** for a tick next to the third option: I used the internet to discover more about insects. | 1m |
| 32 G5 | **Award 1 mark** for a tick next to the first option: We had chicken, pizza and ice cream for dinner. | 1m |
| 33 G5 | **Award 1 mark** for writing any from: *(a pair of) commas, (a pair) of dashes*. | 1m |
| 34 G5 | **Award 1 mark** for a tick next to the first option: I find jigsaws tricky – there are so many pieces. | 1m |
| 35 G6 | **Award 1 mark** for a tick next to the second option: trip | 1m |
| 36 G1 | **Award 1 mark** for *definitely* circled. | 1m |
| 37 G5 | **Award 1 mark** for a tick next to the first option: Ella imagined Jimmy was a frog. | 1m |
| 38 G7 | **Award 1 mark** for a tick next to the first option: My parents request that you attend my party. | 1m |
| 39 G6 | **Award 1 mark** for *ancient* and *modern* circled. | 1m |

Year 6: Autumn Half Term Test 1 – Mark scheme

| Qu. | Requirement | Mark |
|---|---|---|
| 40 G6 | **Award 1 mark** for *il* written in the box. | 1m |
| 41 G5 | **Award 1 mark** for a tick in the second box. | 1m |
| 42 G7 | **Award 2 marks** for all three words circled correctly, **award 1 mark** for two words circled correctly: <br><br> *requests, recognise, achievements* | 2m |
| 43 G5 | **Award 2 marks** for all three boxes ticked correctly, **award 1 mark** for two boxes ticked correctly: <br><br> The giraffe's neck is very long. = Possessive <br> A lion's mane is extremely furry. = Possessive <br> The elephants wandered across the savannah. = Plural | 2m |
| 44 G6 | **a) Award 1 mark** for any suitable explanation, for example *a word with a similar meaning*. <br> **b) Award 1 mark** for any suitable synonym, for example: *messy, dishevelled, chaotic*. | 2m |

# Mark scheme for Autumn Half Term 2

| Qu. | Requirement | Mark |
|---|---|---|
| 1<br>G5 | **Award 1 mark** for *United Kingdom, England, Scotland, Wales* and *Northern Ireland* circled. | 1m |
| 2<br>G5 | **Award 1 mark** for *dog's* circled | 1m |
| 3<br>G4 | **Award 1 mark** for *Miss Reed is tidying the school library.* written on the line. | 1m |
| 4<br>G6 | **Award 1 mark** for *friendship* written in the box. | 1m |
| 5<br>G1 | **Award 1 mark** for *After lunch, Class 6 had Maths.* written on the line. | 1m |
| 6<br>G7 | **Award 1 mark** for a tick next to the fourth option: Archie did the watering. | 1m |
| 7<br>G5 | **Award 1 mark** for *Evan, Thomas, Smalltown, Primary* and *School* circled. | 1m |
| 8<br>G7 | **Award 1 mark** for a tick next to the first option: I went to the football match with my uncle. | 1m |
| 9<br>G4 | **Award 1 mark** for the sentence written correctly using the past progressive: Callum was trying to read his book. | 1m |
| 10<br>G1 | **Award 1 mark** a tick next to the second option: as a fronted adverbial | 1m |
| 11<br>G1 G6 | **Award 1 mark** for *in* written in the box. | 1m |
| 12<br>G4 | **Award 1 mark** for a tick next to the second option: have played | 1m |
| 13<br>G5 | **Award 2 marks** for all three boxes ticked correctly, **award 1 mark** for two boxes ticked correctly:<br>The teachers' mugs were in the staffroom. = Plural<br>The princess's crowns were covered in jewels. = Singular<br>Those are the girls' toys. = Plural | 2m |
| 14<br>G7 | **Award 1 mark** for the sentence written correctly: Gurdip did the drawing. | 1m |
| 15<br>G5 | **Award 1 mark** for a tick in the third box. | 1m |
| 16<br>G4 | **Award 1 mark** for *were* circled. | 1m |
| 17<br>G6 | **Award 1 mark** for *microphone* written on the line. | 1m |
| 18<br>G4 | **Award 2 marks** for all three boxes ticked correctly, **award 1 mark** for two boxes ticked correctly:<br>The children are playing in the playground. = Present progressive<br>Donal has finished his reading book. = Present perfect<br>I am walking to school. = Present progressive | 2m |
| 19<br>G5 | **Award 1 mark** for *sisters'* circled. | 1m |
| 20<br>G6 | **Award 1 mark** for a tick next to the fourth option: chilly | 1m |

Year 6: Autumn Half Term Test 2 – Mark scheme

| Qu. | Requirement | Mark |
|---|---|---|
| 21 G7 | **Award 1 mark** for *is* written in the box. | 1m |
| 22 G4 | **Award 2 marks** for all three boxes ticked correctly, **award 1 mark** for two boxes ticked correctly: <br> Zara is baking some cakes for her friends. = Yes <br> Ali's eating the cakes. = Yes <br> Sasha didn't want any cakes. = No | 2m |
| 23 G6 | **Award 1 mark** for *helpful* written on the line. | 1m |
| 24 G1 | **Award 1 mark** for a tick next to the second option: <u>One day last week,</u> we went to town. | 1m |
| 25 G4 | **Award 1 mark** for *has eaten* written in the box. | 1m |
| 26 G1 | **Award 1 mark** for a tick next to the first option: as a fronted adverbial. | 1m |
| 27 G1 | **Award 1 mark** for *he* and *it* written in the boxes. | 1m |
| 28 G1 | **Award 1 mark** for *his*, *hers* and *theirs* written on the lines. | 1m |
| 29 G5 | **Award 1 mark** for a semi-colon placed after the word *later*. | 1m |
| 30 G1 | **Award 1 mark** for a tick next to the second option: pronoun | 1m |
| 31 G1 | **Award 1 mark** for *yours* circled. | 1m |
| 32 G5 | **Award 1 mark** for *boys'* written in the box. | 1m |
| 33 G5 | **Award 1 mark** for a tick in the third box, after *test*. | 1m |
| 34 G5 | **Award 1 mark** for a hyphen placed between *well* and *known*: I have a collection of well-known traditional tales on my bookshelf. | 1m |
| 35 G4 | **Award 1 mark** for a tick next to the fourth option: has finished | 1m |
| 36 G5 | **Award 1 mark** for a tick next to the first option: Sam has some little-used toys in his cupboard. | 1m |
| 37 G7 | **Award 1 mark** for *were* circled. | 1m |
| 38 G5 | **Award 1 mark** for a tick next to the fourth option: The children like these games: Ludo, chess and cards. | 1m |
| 39 G7 | **Award 2 marks** for all three boxes ticked correctly, **award 1 mark** for two boxes ticked correctly: <br> I wish I was going to the cinema at the weekend. = Incorrect <br> It is important that the class sit down. = Correct <br> If I were older, I'd like to join the police force. = Correct. | 2m |
| 40 G5 | **Award 1 mark** for a tick next to the second option: Six-foot soldiers guarded the queen. | 1m |
| 41 G5 | **Award 1 mark** for a hyphen placed between *well* and *liked*: Zoe is a well-liked member of Class 6. | 1m |
| 42 G7 | **Award 1 mark** for *were being* written in the box. | 1m |

| Qu. | Requirement | Mark |
|---|---|---|
| 43<br>G6 | **Award 1 mark** for *noon* and *midday* circled. | 1m |
| 44<br>G7 | **Award 1 mark** for *were* circled. | 1m |
| 45<br>G5 | **Award 1 mark** for a colon and two semi-colons placed correctly: Children need to bring the following on the school trip: a waterproof coat; sensible walking shoes; and their pencils. | 1m |
| 46<br>G5 | **Award 1 mark** for a response that demonstrates understanding of the plural possessive apostrophe, e.g.<br>• In the second sentence, it means there is only one sister.<br>• In the first one, it shows plural possession.<br>• 1. Two sisters. 2. One sister.<br>**Also accept** responses that demonstrate understanding without referring to the second sentence, e.g.<br>In the first sentence, there is more than one sister.<br>**There are no spelling or punctuation requirements for this question.** | 1m |

Year 6: Spring Half Term Test 1 – Mark scheme

# Mark scheme for Spring Half Term 1

| Qu. | Requirement | Mark |
|---|---|---|
| 1<br>G5 | **Award 1 mark** for two full stops added correctly: The spider scuttled across the floor. I could see it beneath the sofa. | 1m |
| 2<br>G1 | **Award 2 marks** for ticks next to the first, third and fourth options.<br>**Award 1 mark** for two boxes ticked correctly. | 2m |
| 3<br>G5 | **Award 1 mark** for inverted commas added correctly to the sentence: Suki shouted, "Quick! Look at the baby bird." | 1m |
| 4<br>G5 | **Award 1 mark** for a comma (,) written in the box. | 1m |
| 5<br>G1 G6 | **Award 1 mark** for *in* written in the box. | 1m |
| 6<br>G5 | **Award 1 mark** for a tick next to the first option: Joe opened his lunchbox. He took out a sandwich and ate it. | 1m |
| 7<br>G4 | **Award 2 marks** for all three boxes ticked correctly, **award 1 mark** for two boxes ticked correctly:<br>The dog is chasing a stick. = Present progressive<br>The cat was sleeping on a chair. = Past progressive<br>The bird was resting on a branch. = Past progressive | 2m |
| 8<br>G1 | **Award 1 mark** for a tick in the box under *certainly*. | 1m |
| 9<br>G5 | **Award 1 mark** for the sentence written on the line with capital letters and full stops inserted correctly: The cat slept in the armchair. It was curled up in a ball. | 1m |
| 10<br>G5 | **Award 1 mark** for a semi-colon inserted correctly: It's snowing; I'm so excited! | 1m |
| 11<br>G4 | **Award 1 mark** for a tick next to the second option: Angus was drawing in his sketch book. | 1m |
| 12<br>G5 | **Award 1 mark** for explaining that the capital letters are used to indicate the names of people, places and months. Accept reference to proper nouns. | 1m |
| 13<br>G5 | **Award 1 mark** for a pair of commas inserted correctly: Anna, a girl in our class, is from Poland. | 1m |
| 14<br>G4 | **Award 1 mark** for *Mrs Chan was walking to school this morning.* written on the line | 1m |
| 15<br>G7 | **Award 1 mark** for a tick next to the first option: The children made an incredible discovery today. | 1m |
| 16<br>G5 | **Award 1 mark** for a pair of brackets inserted correctly: Mr Jones (our teacher) is really funny. | 1m |
| 17<br>G4 | **Award 1 mark** for a tick next to the third option: past progressive | 1m |
| 18<br>G1 G6 | **Award 1 mark** for *kills* and *destroys* circled. | 1m |
| 19<br>G5 | **Award 1 mark** for ticks in the second and fourth boxes. | 1m |
| 20<br>G3 | **Award 1 mark** for a tick next to the third option: an expanded noun phrase. | 1m |
| 21<br>G5 | **Award 1 mark** for any from: (a pair of) commas, (a pair) of dashes. | 1m |

# Year 6: Spring Half Term Test 1 – Mark scheme

| Qu. | Requirement | Mark |
|---|---|---|
| 22 G5 | **Award 1 mark** for writing direct speech correctly: *I said, "I wanted to take the shortcut."* or *I said, "I want to take the shortcut."* | 1m |
| 23 G3 | **Award 1 mark** for any reasonable preposition phrase, for example: *with loud voices, in unison, in the hall, under the big tree, on the stage.* | 1m |
| 24 G5 | **Award 1 mark** for a comma inserted correctly: Once we got home, we had a drink of juice and a biscuit. | 1m |
| 25 G1 | **Award 1 mark** for any reasonable fronted adverbial written on the line, for example: *Earlier today, Quickly and carefully, In the kitchen.* | 1m |
| 26 G5 | **Award 1 mark** for a colon inserted correctly: There are two places that I have always wanted to visit: New York and Paris. | 1m |
| 27 G5 | **Award 1 mark** for parenthesis (pairs of commas, dashes or brackets) added correctly to the sentence, for example: Sophie's mum, who is our school cook, bakes the best cookies ever. | 1m |
| 28 G1 | **Award 1 mark** for any adverb from: *probably, definitely, clearly, obviously, certainly.* | 1m |
| 29 G4 | **Award 2 marks** for all three boxes ticked correctly, **award 1 mark** for two boxes ticked correctly: <br> Everyone played on the field. = Active <br> The bread was baked by the baker. = Passive <br> The whistle was blown by Mr Gee. = Passive. | 2m |
| 30 G1 | **Award 1 mark** for *certainly* circled. | 1m |
| 31 G5 | **Award 1 mark** for a comma inserted correctly: After a long day at school, I lay on my bed and read my book. | 1m |
| 32 G1 G6 | **Award 1 mark** for *un* written in the box. | 1m |
| 33 G5 | **Award 1 mark** for a colon (:) written in the box. | 1m |
| 34 G4 | **Award 1 mark** for *The football was chased by the children.* written on the line. | 1m |
| 35 G7 | **Award 1 mark** for a tick next to the second option: Spending too much time on a computer should be avoided. | 1m |
| 36 G3 | **Award 1 mark** for a tick next to the third option: as a preposition phrase | 1m |
| 37 G5 | **Award 1 mark** for a semi-colon inserted correctly: Anita was a great rugby player; she scored lots of points. | 1m |
| 38 G5 | **Award 1 mark** for a tick next to the fourth option: semi-colon | 1m |
| 39 G7 | **Award 2 marks** for all three words circled correctly, **award 1 mark** for two words circled correctly: <br> *invited, inform, commence* | 2m |
| 40 G4 | **Award 2 marks** for all three boxes ticked correctly, **award 1 mark** for two boxes ticked correctly: <br> Everyone played chase. = Active <br> The book was read by the teacher. = Passive <br> The parcel was delivered by the post lady. = Passive | 2m |
| 41 G1 | **Award 1 mark** for *clearly* written in the box. | 1m |
| 42 G5 | **Award 1 mark** for *Mr Smith said, "Put on your coats."* written on the line. | 1m |

Year 6: Spring Half Term Test 1 – Mark scheme

| Qu. | Requirement | Mark |
|---|---|---|
| 43<br>G1 G6 | **Award 1 mark** for *worthless* and *valuable* both circled. | 1m |
| 44<br>G4 | **Award 1 mark** for *The children broke the window.* written on the line. | 1m |
| 45<br>G5 | **Award 1 mark** for each item placed on a separate line with lowercase letters used throughout. Accept commas or semi-colons at the ends of lines 1 and 2 with a full stop after the final point. | 1m |

# Mark scheme for Spring Half Term 2

| Qu. | Requirement | Mark |
|---|---|---|
| 1<br>G1 | **Award 1 mark** for *the*, *a*, *an* and *a* circled. | 1m |
| 2<br>G5 | **Award 1 mark** for a tick in the second box. | 1m |
| 3<br>G5 | **Award 1 mark** for inverted commas added correctly: Seema announced, "I would like to be a doctor when I grow up." | 1m |
| 4<br>G6 | **Award 1 mark** for *useful* written in the box. | 1m |
| 5<br>G4 | **Award 2 marks** for all three boxes ticked correctly, **award 1 mark** for two boxes ticked correctly:<br>The twins have bathed the dog. = Present perfect<br>Joe has finished his homework. = Present perfect<br>Aliyah is walking to school. = Present progressive | 2m |
| 6<br>G5 | **Award 1 mark** for *school's* circled. | 1m |
| 7<br>G1 | **Award 1 mark** for a tick next to the fourth option: a fronted adverbial | 1m |
| 8<br>G1 | **Award 1 mark** for *a*, *an* and *a* written on the lines. | 1m |
| 9<br>G5 | **Award 1 mark** for a tick next to the fourth option: I have pens, paper, crayons and pencils. | 1m |
| 10<br>G6 | **Award 1 mark** for a tick next to the second option: water | 1m |
| 11<br>G5 | **Award 1 mark** for two commas added correctly: Carlo has an old bus ticket, an elastic band, a sweet wrapper and his front door key in his pocket. | 1m |
| 12<br>G4 | **Award 2 marks** for all three boxes ticked correctly, **award 1 mark** for two boxes ticked correctly:<br>The children have eaten their lunch. = Present perfect<br>Martin has finished his drawing. = Present perfect<br>I had tried my best in the test. = Past perfect | 2m |
| 13<br>G5 | **Award 1 mark** for a colon added correctly: There are two things that I have always wanted: a camera and a telescope. | 1m |
| 14<br>G1 | **Award 1 mark** for *In the summer holidays* underlined. | 1m |
| 15<br>G5 | **Award 1 mark** for a tick in the second box. | 1m |
| 16<br>G7 | **Award 1 mark** for a tick next to the first option: I went to the cinema with my sister. | 1m |
| 17<br>G1 G6 | **Award 1 mark** for *un* written in the box. | 1m |
| 18<br>G7 | **Award 1 mark** for all three words circled correctly:<br>*is, are, is* | 1m |
| 19<br>G5 | **Award 1 mark** for the sentence rewritten correctly: "It's important to be quiet in the library," whispered Miss Lane / Miss Lane whispered. | 1m |
| 20<br>G3 | **Award 1 mark** for *that is shiny and blue* underlined. | 1m |

Year 6: Spring Half Term Test 2 – Mark scheme

| Qu. | Requirement | Mark |
|---|---|---|
| 21 G4 | **Award 1 mark** for *can* written in the box. | 1m |
| 22 G1 | **Award 1 mark** for the sentence rewritten with a fronted adverbial: By the time the sun comes up, our postman has already delivered our post. | 1m |
| 23 G7 | **Award 1 mark** for *were* circled. | 1m |
| 24 G5 | **Award 2 marks** for all three boxes ticked correctly, **award 1 mark** for two boxes ticked correctly: <br> The girls' books were kept on a shelf. = Plural <br> The princess's shoes were covered in mud. = Singular <br> The boys' football boots were left by the door. = Plural | 2m |
| 25 G5 | **Award 1 mark** for the sentence rewritten correctly: "Would you like to come to my party?" asked Sophie. | 1m |
| 26 G3 | **Award 1 mark** for a tick next to the second option: Whose | 1m |
| 27 G3 | **Award 1 mark** for a tick in the first box. | 1m |
| 28 G4 | **Award 1 mark** for either *may* or *might* written on the line | 1m |
| 29 G5 | **Award 1 mark** for a tick next to the second option: These are my favourite animals: mice, snakes and spiders. | 1m |
| 30 G4 | **Award 1 mark** for all three modal verbs circled correctly: <br> *should, can, might* | 1m |
| 31 G5 | **Award 1 mark** for a comma added to the sentence correctly: After leaving Jimmy, Jo and Fergal went to the theatre. | 1m |
| 32 G5 | **Award 1 mark** for a tick next to the third option: Our class can get quite noisy – there are so many children. | 1m |
| 33 G5 | **Award 1 mark** for a tick in the second box. | 1m |
| 34 G5 | **Award 2 marks** for all three boxes ticked correctly, **award 1 mark** for two boxes ticked correctly: <br> The bad-tempered child was misbehaving. = Correct <br> The footpath was dog-friendly. = Correct <br> The ice-cream-cone was toffee flavoured. = Incorrect | 2m |
| 35 G4 | **Award 1 mark** for the sentence rewritten in the active: The teacher blew the whistle. | 1m |
| 36 G5 | **Award 1 mark** for a hyphen and a comma inserted correctly: My sister is an ice-skating champion, a swimmer and a runner. | 1m |
| 37 G7 | **Award 2 marks** for all three boxes ticked correctly, **award 1 mark** for two boxes ticked correctly: <br> I wish I were able to do a cartwheel. = Correct <br> If I were able, I'd like to compete in the Olympics. = Correct <br> I wish I was going to the circus tonight. = Incorrect. | 2m |

Year 6: Spring Half Term Test 2 – Mark scheme

| Qu. | Requirement | Mark |
|---|---|---|
| 38 G5 | **Award 1 mark** for a response that demonstrates understanding of the plural possessive apostrophe, e.g.<br>• In the second sentence, it means there is more than one sister.<br>• In the first one, it shows plural possession.<br>• 1. One sister. 2. Two sisters.<br>**Also accept** responses that demonstrate understanding without referring to the second sentence, e.g.<br>In the first sentence, there is only one sister.<br>**There are no spelling or punctuation requirements for this question.** | 1m |
| 39 G5 | **Award 1 mark** for a colon and two semi-colons inserted correctly: At the safari park, you can see: groups of children; families of monkeys; and a pride of lions. | 1m |
| 40 G6 | **Award 1 mark** for a tick next to the second option: begin | 1m |
| 41 G4 | **Award 2 marks** for all three boxes ticked correctly, **award 1 mark** for two boxes ticked correctly:<br>The alien was found by the children. = Passive<br>Everyone watched the film. = Active<br>Yoko was doing a painting. = Active | 2m |
| 42 G5 | **Award 1 mark** for a comma and a dash inserted in the sentence correctly: This weekend, I am going to get a dog – the first I have ever owned. | 1m |
| 43 G5 | **Award 1 mark** for explaining that in the first sentence the comma indicates that travellers are worried about getting lost. In the second sentence, the omission of the comma indicates that it is people who travel in time that are worried about getting lost. | 1m |
| 44 G4 | **Award 1 mark** for any correctly punctuated sentence using the passive voice, for example: *The apples were picked by the farmer. The children were given awards.* | 1m |

Year 6: Summer Half Term Test 1 – Mark scheme

# Mark scheme for Summer Half Term 1

| Qu. | Requirement | Mark |
|---|---|---|
| 1 G5 | **Award 1 mark** for *logan*, *sasha*, *victor* and *amy* circled. | 1m |
| 2 G5 | **Award 1 mark** for a tick in the third box. | 1m |
| 3 G1 | **Award 1 mark** for *the*, *a*, *a* and *an* circled. | 1m |
| 4 G1 | **Award 1 mark** for a tick in the second box. | 1m |
| 5 G5 | **Award 1 mark** for all four lines drawn correctly:<br>they have = they've<br>do not = don't<br>we will = we'll<br>it is = it's | 1m |
| 6 G5 | **Award 1 mark** for *eva* and *hanna* circled. | 1m |
| 7 G4 | **Award 1 mark** for *was* circled. | 1m |
| 8 G5 | **Award 1 mark** for two commas added correctly: Olga has a pencil, a pen, some coloured crayons and a ruler in her pencil case. | 1m |
| 9 G5 | **Award 1 mark** for *let us*, *I will* and *they would* written in the boxes. | 1m |
| 10 G1 | **Award 1 mark** for a tick next to the fourth option: adjective | 1m |
| 11 G5 | **Award 1 mark** for *I'd* circled. | 1m |
| 12 G1 | **Award 1 mark** for a tick in the third box. | 1m |
| 13 G1 | **Award 1 mark** for *and*, *or* and *but* written on the lines. | 1m |
| 14 G4 | **Award 1 mark** for a tick next to the third option: is playing | 1m |
| 15 G1 | **Award 1 mark** for *before* written in the box. | 1m |
| 16 G1 | **Award 1 mark** for all three lines drawn correctly:<br>Mum bought me <u>an</u> ice-cream.<br>It had <u>a</u> chocolate flake in the top.<br><u>The</u> cone was toffee flavoured. | 1m |
| 17 G4 | **Award 1 mark** for the sentence rewritten in the present progressive: Mr Hooper is teaching the children how to multiply decimal fractions. | 1m |
| 18 G1 | **Award 1 mark** for *a*, *an* and *a* written in the boxes. | 1m |
| 19 G1 G6 | **Award 1 mark** for *pre* written in the box. | 1m |
| 20 G5 | **Award 1 mark** for *couldn't* written on the line. | 1m |

# Year 6: Summer Half Term Test 1 – Mark scheme

| Qu. | Requirement | Mark |
|---|---|---|
| 21 G1 G6 | **Award 1 mark** for *anti* written in the box. | 1m |
| 22 G1 G6 | **Award 1 mark** for all four lines drawn correctly: *prehistoric, submarine, autobiography, supersonic* | 1m |
| 23 G1 | **Award 1 mark** for a suitable preposition written in the box, for example: *beneath, inside, behind, under.* | 1m |
| 24 G1 | **Award 1 mark** for a tick next to the third option: at | 1m |
| 25 G4 | **Award 2 marks** for all three boxes ticked correctly, **award 1 mark** for two boxes ticked correctly: <br> Ravi was doing a handstand. = Past progressive <br> Lucy skipped in the playground. = Simple past <br> Hamid was doing a puzzle. = Past progressive | 2m |
| 26 G1 | **Award 1 mark** for the sentence rewritten with a fronted adverbial: Next week, Class 6 will be performing their play to the school. | 1m |
| 27 G1 | **Award 2 marks** for all three boxes ticked correctly, **award 1 mark** for two boxes ticked correctly: <br> Gus had a shiny bike. = Adjective <br> The bike had big wheels. = Adjective <br> Gus rode the bike quickly. = Adverb | 2m |
| 28 G3 | **Award 2 marks** for ticks next to the first, second and third options. <br> **Award 1 mark** for two boxes ticked correctly. | 2m |
| 29 G3 | **Award 1 mark** for any suitable adjective written on the line, for example: *cute, cuddly, furry, lovely.* | 1m |
| 30 G4 | **Award 2 marks** for all three boxes ticked correctly, **award 1 mark** for two boxes ticked correctly: <br> The teacher read the story. = Active <br> The cake was made by the baker. = Passive <br> Nina was watching a film. = Active | 2m |
| 31 G1 | **Award 1 mark** for the sentence written with a fronted adverbial: After school, Ravi and Joshi went to the park with their aunty. | 1m |
| 32 G1 G6 | **Award 1 mark** for a tick next to the second option: take apart | 1m |
| 33 G7 | **Award 1 mark** for a tick next to the first option: It's important to be punctual. | 1m |
| 34 G1 G6 | **Award 1 mark** for all four lines drawn correctly: *impossible, inanimate, overrule, misjudge* | 1m |
| 35 G6 | **Award 1 mark** for *mismatched* written in the box. | 1m |
| 36 G5 | **Award 1 mark** for a semi-colon inserted correctly: I'll play with you tomorrow; I have to go to my gran's house right now. | 1m |
| 37 G7 | **Award 1 mark** for a tick next to the fourth option: Please enter the school by the front entrance. | 1m |
| 38 G4 | **Award 1 mark** for the sentence rewritten in the active: The engineer repaired the machine. | 1m |
| 39 G1 G6 | **Award 1 mark** for *de* written in the box. | 1m |

Year 6: Summer Half Term Test 1 – Mark scheme

| Qu. | Requirement | Mark |
|---|---|---|
| 40 G5 | **Award 1 mark** for a tick next to the first option: I like these fruits: apples, oranges and pears. | 1m |
| 41 G4 | **Award 1 mark** for the sentence rewritten in the passive: The book was read by the teacher. | 1m |
| 42 G5 | **Award 1 mark** for a colon inserted correctly: My favourite colour is red: it is the colour of my favourite football team. | 1m |
| 43 G6 | **Award 1 mark** for a tick next to the third option: exhale | 1m |
| 44 G5 | **Award 1 mark** for a dash inserted correctly: All the children wore the same – blue blazers and stripy ties. | 1m |
| 45 G6 | **Award 1 mark** for *slash* and *Cutting* circled. | 1m |
| 46 G1 G6 | **Award 1 mark** for *dis* written in the box. | 1m |

# Mark scheme for Summer Half Term 2

| Qu. | Requirement | Mark |
|---|---|---|
| 1 G5 | **Award 1 mark** for *jamal, london, buckingham palace* and *trafalgar square* circled. | 1m |
| 2 G1 | **Award 1 mark** for *because* circled. | 1m |
| 3 G5 | **Award 1 mark** for explaining that the capital letters are for months, names and proper nouns (or places). | 1m |
| 4 G5 | **Award 1 mark** for an apostrophe added correctly: I have borrowed Donal's football. | 1m |
| 5 G6 | **Award 1 mark** for *behaviour* written in the box. | 1m |
| 6 G5 | **Award 1 mark** for a tick next to the third option: I waited at the bus stop. Eventually, the bus came and I got on. | 1m |
| 7 G4 | **Award 1 mark** for *James and David were playing football at the weekend.* written on the line. | 1m |
| 8 G5 | **Award 1 mark** for *Seema's* circled. | 1m |
| 9 G1 | **Award 1 mark** for a tick next to the first option: therefore | 1m |
| 10 G4 | **Award 1 mark** for a tick next to the third option: past progressive | 1m |
| 11 G6 | **Award 1 mark** for a tick next to the fourth option: time | 1m |
| 12 G4 | **Award 2 marks** for all three boxes ticked correctly, **award 1 mark** for two boxes ticked correctly:<br>Jo had played outside all afternoon. = Past perfect<br>I have walked ten miles for charity. = Present perfect<br>The dog has eaten my homework! = Present perfect | 2m |
| 13 G3 | **Award 1 mark** for *expanded noun phrase* written on the line.<br>**Also accept** *noun phrase*. | 1m |
| 14 G5 | **Award 1 mark** for *boy's* circled. | 1m |
| 15 G5 | **Award 1 mark** for inverted commas added correctly: Sam shouted, "Pass the ball! Pass the ball, quick!" | 1m |
| 16 G7 | **Award 1 mark** for *We were looking forward to our trip to the zoo.* written on the line. | 1m |
| 17 G3 | **Award 1 mark** for any reasonable noun phrase formed with a preposition, for example: *with a nut for its dinner; in a forest, by digging in its claws.* | 1m |
| 18 G1 | **Award 1 mark** for *theirs*, *hers* and *yours* written on the lines. | 1m |
| 19 G5 | **Award 1 mark** for the sentence punctuated correctly with speech punctuation:<br>Bryn said, "I am going to watch United play City at the weekend."<br>**Also accept** "I am going to watch United play City at the weekend," said Bryn / Bryn said. | 1m |
| 20 G5 | **Award 1 mark** for *neighbours'* circled. | 1m |

Year 6: Summer Half Term Test 2 – Mark scheme

| Qu. | Requirement | Mark |
|---|---|---|
| 21 G1 | **Award 1 mark** for a tick next to the second option: pronoun | 1m |
| 22 G1 G6 | **Award 1 mark** for the suffix *ate* written on the line. | 1m |
| 23 G5 | **Award 1 mark** for a tick in the first box. | 1m |
| 24 G3 | **Award 1 mark** for *that* circled. | 1m |
| 25 G4 | **Award 1 mark** for *may*, *might* or *could* written on the line. | 1m |
| 26 G1 | **Award 1 mark** for any sentence that starts with a fronted adverbial that is followed by a comma. | 1m |
| 27 G1 G6 | a) **Award 1 mark** for all three lines drawn correctly: *hospitalise, captivate, intensify*<br>b) **Award 1 mark** for each word written on the line correctly. Accept no spelling errors. | 2m |
| 28 G5 | **Award 1 mark** for a response that demonstrates understanding of the plural possessive apostrophe, e.g.<br>• In the second sentence, it means there is only one cow.<br>• In the first one, it shows plural possession.<br>• 1. Many cows. 2. One cow.<br>**Also accept** responses that demonstrate understanding without referring to the second sentence, e.g.<br>In the first sentence, there is more than one cow.<br>**There are no spelling or punctuation requirements for this question.** | 1m |
| 29 G3 | **Award 1 mark** for *that is white and black* underlined. | 1m |
| 30 G1 | **Award 1 mark** for *Perhaps* circled. | 1m |
| 31 G5 | **Award 1 mark** for parenthesis added correctly: While walking to school, James Arnold – a pupil from St Mary's Primary – rescued a kitten from a tree.<br>**Also accept** a pair of brackets in the same positions. | 1m |
| 32 G4 | **Award 1 mark** for explaining that in the second sentence there is less certainty that the class will go to the zoo.<br>**Also accept** answers that refer to the first sentence, for example: *In the first sentence the class are definitely going to the zoo, but it is less likely in the second sentence.* | 1m |
| 33 G4 | **Award 2 marks** for all three boxes ticked correctly, **award 1 mark** for two boxes ticked correctly:<br>The chair was broken. = Passive<br>The dog was walked by its owner. = Passive<br>The cat was sleeping. = Active | 2m |
| 34 G5 | **Award 1 mark** for a tick next to the first option: "May I paint Miss Sohal?" asked Jimmy. | 1m |
| 35 G7 | **Award 1 mark** for a tick next to the fourth option: were | 1m |
| 36 G7 | **Award 1 mark** for *were* circled. | 1m |
| 37 G5 | **Award 1 mark** for a tick next to the first option: I really struggle with maths – it's just so confusing. | 1m |

Year 6: Summer Half Term Test 2 – Mark scheme

| Qu. | Requirement | Mark |
|---|---|---|
| 38 G1 G6 | a) **Award 1 mark** for explaining that an antonym is a word with an opposite meaning to a given word.<br>b) **Award 1 mark** for writing a suitable antonym to calm, for example: *harsh, rough, fierce, agitated.* | 2m |
| 39 G5 | **Award 1 mark** for a hyphen inserted correctly: My parents like the restaurant because it has a child-friendly atmosphere. | 1m |
| 40 G4 | **Award 1 mark** for the sentence written on the line correctly: The children put away the toys. / The children put the toys away. | 1m |
| 41 G5 | **Award 1 mark** for a semi-colon inserted correctly: I have a new bag; it has red spots and a green strap. | 1m |
| 42 G7 | **Award 1 mark** for a tick next to the first option: We request that pupils wear school uniform at all times. | 1m |
| 43 G5 | **Award 1 mark** for a colon and two semi-colons inserted correctly: On her desk, Mrs Cooper has the following items: a stapler; a pot of pencils; and an apple. | 1m |
| 44 G5 | **Award 1 mark** for each item placed on a separate line with lowercase letters used throughout. Accept commas or semi-colons at the ends of lines 1 and 2 with a full stop after the final point. | 1m |
| 45 G5 | **Award 1 mark** for explaining that in the second sentence there are some ropes that are five metres long.<br>**Also accept** reference to the first sentence, for example: *In the first sentence there are five ropes that are a metre long and in the second sentence there are some ropes that are five metres long.* | 1m |
| 46 G7 | **Award 1 mark** for a correctly punctuated sentence using the subjunctive, for example: *If I were a time-traveller, I'd visit the dinosaurs. I wish I were really rich so that I could buy a racing car.* | 1m |

Year 6: Record Sheet

| Name: | Class: |

## Year 6 Grammar, Punctuation and Vocabulary Record Sheet

| Tests | Mark | Total marks | Key skills to target |
|---|---|---|---|
| Autumn Half Term Test 1 | | | |
| Autumn Half Term Test 2 | | | |
| Spring Half Term Test 1 | | | |
| Spring Half Term Test 2 | | | |
| Summer Half Term Test 1 | | | |
| Summer Half Term Test 2 | | | |

www.ingramcontent.com/pod-product-compliance
Lightning Source LLC
Chambersburg PA
CBHW081418300426
44109CB00019BA/2345